COUNCIL *on*
FOREIGN
RELATIONS

Council Special Report No. 86
May 2020

The End of World Order and American Foreign Policy

Robert D. Blackwill and Thomas Wright

The Council on Foreign Relations (CFR) is an independent, nonpartisan membership organization, think tank, and publisher dedicated to being a resource for its members, government officials, business executives, journalists, educators and students, civic and religious leaders, and other interested citizens in order to help them better understand the world and the foreign policy choices facing the United States and other countries. Founded in 1921, CFR carries out its mission by maintaining a diverse membership, with special programs to promote interest and develop expertise in the next generation of foreign policy leaders; convening meetings at its headquarters in New York and in Washington, DC, and other cities where senior government officials, members of Congress, global leaders, and prominent thinkers come together with Council members to discuss and debate major international issues; supporting a Studies Program that fosters independent research, enabling CFR scholars to produce articles, reports, and books and hold roundtables that analyze foreign policy issues and make concrete policy recommendations; publishing *Foreign Affairs*, the preeminent journal on international affairs and U.S. foreign policy; sponsoring Independent Task Forces that produce reports with both findings and policy prescriptions on the most important foreign policy topics; and providing up-to-date information and analysis about world events and American foreign policy on its website, CFR.org.

The Council on Foreign Relations takes no institutional positions on policy issues and has no affiliation with the U.S. government. All views expressed in its publications and on its website are the sole responsibility of the author or authors.

Council Special Reports (CSRs) are concise policy briefs, produced to provide a rapid response to a developing crisis or contribute to the public's understanding of current policy dilemmas. CSRs are written by individual authors—who may be CFR fellows or acknowledged experts from outside the institution—in consultation with an advisory committee, and are intended to take sixty days from inception to publication. The committee serves as a sounding board and provides feedback on a draft report. It usually meets twice—once before a draft is written and once again when there is a draft for review; however, advisory committee members, unlike Task Force members, are not asked to sign off on the report or to otherwise endorse it. Once published, CSRs are posted on CFR.org.

For further information about CFR or this Special Report, please write to the Council on Foreign Relations, 58 East 68th Street, New York, NY 10065, or call the Communications office at 212.434.9888. Visit our website, CFR.org.

To submit a letter in response to a Council Special Report for publication on our website, CFR.org, you may send an email to publications@cfr.org. Alternatively, letters may be mailed to us at: Publications Department, Council on Foreign Relations, 58 East 68th Street, New York, NY 10065. Letters should include the writer's name, postal address, and daytime phone number. Letters may be edited for length and clarity, and may be published online. Please do not send attachments. All letters become the property of the Council on Foreign Relations and will not be returned. We regret that, owing to the volume of correspondence, we cannot respond to every letter.

CONTENTS

FOREWORD

World order is a fundamental concept of international relations. At its core, world order is a description and a measure of the world's condition at a particular moment or over a specified period of time. It tends to reflect the degree to which there are widely accepted rules as to how international relations ought to be carried out and the degree to which there is a balance of power to buttress those rules so that those who disagree with them are not tempted to violate them or are likely to fail if in fact they do. Any measure of order necessarily includes elements of both order and disorder and the balance between them.

Until recently, articles and books explicitly examining world order have been few in number, principally because for the past seventy-five years world order was clearly defined. During the Cold War, the order was bipolar, split between American- and Soviet-led camps. A balance of power, bolstered by nuclear deterrence, kept the central peace, and shared understandings (mostly implicit) of the legitimate aims of foreign policy circumscribed the behavior of both superpowers. Following the Cold War's end and the Soviet Union's collapse some three decades ago, a U.S.-led world order prevailed, underpinned by American absolute economic and military strengths and relative advantage over others. Now, however, against the backdrop of a retrenching United States, a rising China, a resentful and assertive Russia, a nuclear North Korea, and an ambitious Iran, not to mention a number of serious global challenges, much of what had been assumed can no longer be taken for granted. Both the balance of power and the consensus at the heart of world orders has faded.

At this moment of uncertainty and potential transition, accelerated by the ongoing COVID-19 pandemic, Robert D. Blackwill, the Henry A. Kissinger senior fellow for U.S. foreign policy here at the Council on Foreign Relations, and Thomas Wright, the director of the Center on the United States and Europe and a senior fellow at the Brookings Institution, present this new Council Special Report, *The End of World Order and American Foreign Policy*. The report is both analytical and prescriptive. As regards the former, the authors note that along with U.S.-Soviet competition and the Cold War, the COVID-19 pandemic represents the most serious challenge to the U.S.-led international order. They call this "a moment of radical international uncertainty" that "occurs at a troubling time geopolitically, including the withdrawal of the United States from global leadership."

Blackwill and Wright present the case that the old order has given way to multiple orders, which in effect is disorder. "The world has moved away from a Kissingerian standard of world order, in which nations work within the same set of constraints and aspire to meet the same set of rules, toward a model where many countries choose their own paths to order, without much reference to the views of others." More specifically, the two argue the pandemic has undermined order by straining governments, dividing societies, exacerbating societal inequalities, heightening tensions between the United States and China, and demonstrating the vast gap between global problems and the world's ability to address them through existing international institutions.

The authors go on to provide recommendations that would allow the United States to "preserve its national interests and its own notion of international order." First, they argue that American foreign policy must begin at home, and the United States needs to focus on improving domestic governance and its economic competitiveness so that the country regains the will and the capacity to play an active role abroad. They then call for the United States to invest in its relations with

Canada and Mexico, develop a more collaborative approach to allies, increase partnership with Europe, upgrade relations with India, invest in international institutions, seek a way to resume engagement with Russia, and focus less on the Middle East and more on Asia. More than anything else, the approach to order advocated here places managing inevitable and growing competition with China at the heart of American diplomacy and its search for order in the world.

I expect what is written in the report about order may be too narrow or too traditional for some readers. This is to be expected. Such debate reflects the reality that this is a moment of real change in the world, coupled with intellectual foment about how to understand it and what to do about it. This Council on Foreign Relations Special Report makes an important, rigorous, and considered contribution to this emerging and critical debate.

Richard N. Haass
President
Council on Foreign Relations
May 2020

ACKNOWLEDGMENTS

This Council Special Report greatly benefited from the dozens of specific suggestions and valuable improvements by Hal Brands, Tarun Chhabra, Francis J. Gavin, Lyndsay Howard, William Inboden, Bruce Jones, Shankar Menon, Lord Charles Powell, Ed Rogers, Dennis Ross, Gary Roughead, Shyam Saran, Jake Sullivan, Stephen M. Walt, Philip Zelikow, and Robert Zoellick. We took many of their suggested fixes but, as they will see, not all. We also thank the speakers and members of the CFR World Order Study Group for their insights during our sessions over the past eight months. To pay attention to smart people always makes one smarter, or, as George Shultz once observed, "Listening is an underrated way of acquiring knowledge." We also thank Council on Foreign Relations (CFR) President Richard N. Haass for his review and comments. We appreciate the work of Patricia Dorff and the CFR Publications team for their editorial contributions. Our special thanks to Daniel Clay for his extensive work on this report.

The analysis and conclusions herein are the authors' responsibility alone.

Robert D. Blackwill and Thomas Wright

INTRODUCTION

Along with U.S.-Soviet competition during the Cold War, COVID-19 is one of the two greatest tests of the U.S.-led international order since its founding over seven decades ago.[1] Nothing else since that time approaches the societal, political, and economic effects of the virus on populations around the world. Not the dozens of violent conflicts that erupted in the international system since 1945. Not the many regional and global economic downturns over the years that reduced the quality of life of ordinary citizens. Not the international effects of the "Time of Troubles" in the United States, from the assassinations, urban riots, and mass demonstrations of 1968, to the presidential resignation in 1974. Not even the two million people who died of smallpox in 1967 in a far less connected world.

At the time of writing, millions are infected globally with millions more likely to come, and hundreds of thousands are dead.[2] Entire populations remain indoors. The International Monetary Fund (IMF) quarterly report *World Economic Outlook* labeled the crisis the Great Lockdown and estimated a reduction in global growth of 3 percent, which makes it the most severe recession since the Great Depression and far worse than the 2008 global financial crisis.[3] Accumulated losses in 2020 and 2021 could reach $9 trillion, which is more than the German and Japanese economies combined. During this crisis, two billion people could fall into abject poverty, half of all jobs in Africa could be lost, oil exports in the Middle East could drop by $250 billion, more than ninety countries could receive aid from the IMF, the number of unemployed people in the United States is over 38.6 million, and the European Union (EU) forecasts the deepest economic recession in its history with EU economies to shrink by 7.4 percent this year.[4] Even as the world goes back to work, any reopening will be partial, with large sectors of society in many nations staying closed. There is a near-consensus among health experts that the crisis will last in one form or another for well over a year, and perhaps longer. The economic and societal consequences will prevail much longer. There will be no V-shaped economic rebound.[5]

This is a moment of radical international uncertainty. Despite many commentaries to the contrary, it is difficult to predict what the long-term impact of the COVID-19 crisis will be on the quest for world order.[6] The last major pandemic, in 1918–19, is not generally judged to have had a major effect on the 1920s and 1930s, but that is likely because it happened in a world already fragmented by World War I.[7] By contrast, although this crisis occurs at a troubling time geopolitically, including the withdrawal of the United States from global leadership, until the pandemic it was a period of interdependence and prosperity for many countries. This plague puts immense strain on individual governments, divides societies, and exacerbates societal inequalities. It encourages leaders to act unilaterally and nationally, rather than in concert. It demonstrates the weaknesses of most international organizations. It exacerbates tensions between the United States and China.[8] It prompts the United States' adversaries to try to take advantage of Washington's tardy and confused reaction to the epidemic.

The crisis poses enveloping international questions. When will the global economy recover? Can Washington and Beijing avoid permanent confrontation with potential catastrophic consequences?[9] Will China advance its national interests at the expense of the United States? Will the U.S. alliance system continue to erode? Will the crisis empower or undermine nationalists and populists? Will the European Union undertake sufficient economic reform that it can retain the allegiance of countries such as Italy by showing that it will be there for all of its member states in a crisis? What will happen in the developing world, where governments have limited health-care capacity and minimal ability to enforce social distancing? Will medical shortcomings trigger mass migration? Will mass digital surveillance become more attractive if it offers an alternative to economic shutdown? These matters are of enormous import, but they are impossible to answer with any confidence at this stage.

The objective of this report is not to predict the long-term consequences of the present crisis (as the American philosopher Yogi Berra stressed, "It's tough to make predictions, especially about the future"). Rather, it is to place this plague in global context. After the Cold War, many observers believed the world's largest powers were converging on a single model of international order—a globalized version of the order the United States had led since the late 1940s. Before Washington's two long wars in the greater Middle East, the rise of China, and the revival of Russia, the 1990s in general was a rare historical decade of a mostly stable, mostly harmonious, and mostly peaceful world order—one that was imperfect and incomplete, but still stood apart from the normal anarchic state of international politics.[10]

This world order period weakened after 9/11 and ended over the past decade, driven by a combination of great power ambition, American withdrawal, and transformational changes that left many nations unmoored from old certainties, "no longer at ease here, in the old dispensation."[11] This report portrays the international situation before the coronavirus struck, posits its current effects on world order, and prescribes what the United States should do about it.

WORLD ORDER
BEFORE COVID-19

To understand the world today, one must first understand the world that came before. We began this project in the fall of 2019 precisely because the world order seemed so troubled. Indeed, for at least six years, since Russia's annexation of Crimea, analysts wrote about the collapse of international order, a tendency that was reinforced by the proliferation of failed states and refugee crises in the Middle East, Brexit, the election of President Donald J. Trump and other populists, the rise of Chinese power and consequent increased rivalry between Washington and Beijing, and a worsening climate.[12] As Robert Kagan put it, the jungle was growing back.[13]

And yet, that the international system is beset by problems and that those difficulties are getting worse is not in itself proof that world order is falling apart. Until COVID-19, global economic growth was strong while poverty continued to decline. The major powers were not on the brink of conflict. With the exception of the Middle East, most of the world's regions were stable. Significant technological breakthroughs improved the lives of billions.[14] So a more fundamental question should be asked: How should world order be defined?

It is helpful to make an initial distinction between international order and world order. International order usually refers to an order led by a specific country, often referring to empire, even though the order in question is not always embraced by all of the world's major powers. The world has had Roman, Byzantine, Mongol, Chinese, French, British, Russian, German, and Japanese orders. In recent decades, international order has become synonymous with the post–World War II order led by the United States—thus Americans, many Europeans, Japanese, Australians, and others believe that the international order includes military alliances, such as the North Atlantic Treaty Organization

(NATO) and bilateral security treaties, and the Group of Seven, even though Russia and China are excluded from all three.

World order, which rarely occurs in history, specifically refers to a shared understanding among the major powers to limit the potential for serious confrontation, including among competitors and adversaries. This report focuses on world order—how much agreement there is between the great powers, particularly those that see themselves as rivals.

In *A World Restored*, Henry Kissinger writes that order and stability result not from a desire to pursue peace or justice, but from a "generally accepted legitimacy" and are "based on an equilibrium of forces." Legitimacy, he says, "means no more than an international agreement about the nature of workable arrangements and about the permissible aims and methods of foreign policy." "It implies," he concludes, "the acceptance of the framework of the international order by all major powers, at least to the extent that no state is so dissatisfied that, like Germany after the Treaty of Versailles, it expresses its dissatisfaction in a revolutionary foreign policy."[15] Kissinger returns to this theme in his 2014 book *World Order*, which he defines as "the concept held by a region or civilization about the nature of just arrangements and the distribution of power thought to be applicable to the entire world." World order rests, he writes, on two components: "a set of commonly accepted rules that define the limits of permissable action and a balance of power that enforces restraint where rules break down."[16]

The Concert of Europe manifested this as a loose set of constraints that moved the major powers beyond a traditional balance of power—no major power would act unilaterally to acquire territory, none would interfere in the domestic governance of others, and none would be humiliated or isolated. The concert was

5

not an agreement of equals. Serving the interests of Great Britain and Russia above all others, it was the mechanism by which the other European powers acquiesced to and sought to influence British and Russian bipolarity.[17]

These mutual constraints gradually fell away in the last quarter of the nineteenth century. They were replaced by a crude balance of power system in Europe that was disrupted and then remade by Chancellor Otto von Bismarck, was weakened with the rise of German imperialism, and collapsed in the years leading up to World War I.[18] An attempt to restore some semblance of world order through the League of Nations failed, and Germany's revolutionary foreign policies of the 1930s and 1940s shattered any prospect of mutual constraint or cooperation among major countries. In the early decades of the Cold War, Americans did not believe in world order as Kissinger defines it. There was, at best, a Western order locked in a bipolar struggle with the Soviet Union. And yet, that bipolar system became a world order of sorts, if that can be understood to mean the gradual acceptance by both superpowers of each other's spheres of influence, their joint opposition to the spread of nuclear weapons, and their desire, especially after 1962, to avert nuclear war.

During his years in office, Kissinger above all else sought to apply his concept and objectives of world order to the relationship between the United States and the Soviet Union and to prepare for the emergence of China as an eventual world power. John Ikenberry, a professor at Princeton University and one of the world's leading liberal theorists of order, argued in the 1990s and 2000s that there is a distinctly liberal logic to order in the post–Cold War period and that the constraints and understandings between the major powers became formalized and institutionalized.[19]

Beginning in the early 1990s, the Cold War order was reconstituted into an aspiring global commonwealth that enlarged NATO and transformed the United Nations, the IMF and the World Bank, the World Trade Organization (WTO), and the EU. The debates on the health of world order usually hinge on whether the United States, China, Russia, or other powers infringe these global rules. They sometimes do—the United States in Kosovo in 1999 and Iraq in 2003; Russia in Georgia in 2008, Ukraine in 2014, and Syria in 2015; and China in the South China Sea and through repeated geoeconomic coercion. Scholars argue about whether these episodes are equivalent or different and how much they represent a general erosion of world order. Experts also focus on whether international institutions, which frequently serve as a proxy for states, can solve or at least manage the wide array of regional and global problems. The answer is usually no, which contributes to endemic pessimism about the current state of world order.

But this assessment of world order may set the bar too high. It is a standard created in the unique moment after the Cold War to describe a world in which the great power rivalry that prevailed for centuries had seemed to evaporate, in which Russia and China were too weak to challenge the United States' international preferences. That unipolar period, if it ever existed, is over.[20] The question is whether the major powers can agree on the fundamental constraints required to establish and sustain a stable world order, or, if such a world order is not possible, they can find another way toward a stable and acceptable geopolitical equilibrium.

THE END OF
WORLD ORDER

Two developments over the past decade ended the post–Cold War world order. The first was a series of decisions by major powers to diverge from the shared understanding of limitations and enforcement that prevailed in the 1990s. The second is profound transformative changes in world affairs—technical, economic, and environmental—that give rise to issues not addressed by post–Cold War world order.

DIVERGENCE

For a decade and a half after the Cold War, the major non-allied powers largely acquiesced to the U.S.-led international order. China and Russia chose not to balance against the United States, partly because it was too far ahead in raw power (what was called unipolarity) and perhaps because they were not yet sufficiently dissatisfied with the status quo.[21] China largely operated within the parameters of the order, and many Americans believed or at least hoped that China would become a responsible stakeholder in it. Russia was more dissatisfied, but there were promising signs—Russian President Dimitri Medvedev spoke the language of economic reform while Washington and Moscow talked of partnership.[22] Brazil and India seemed to be dynamic and multilateralist rising powers that could responsibly add to the foundation of 1990s world order.[23]

Sadly, this century has sharply departed from those U.S.-generated norms.[24] On governance questions, Brazil, Russia, India, China, and South Africa (BRICS) have all regressed.[25] Some observers believe that China has moved toward a totalitarian dictatorship, with President Xi Jinping in power for life as the regime perfects the tools of repression and control with new technologies.[26] Others label the Chinese government as authoritarian. Russian President Vladimir Putin moved Russia in a similar direction, while India's and Brazil's democracies eroded through the decisions of Prime Minister Narendra Modi and President Jair Bolsonaro.

- Russia in 2014 illegally annexed Crimea, the first such act in Europe since World War II and a flagrant violation of the norm against territorial conquest.

- Brazil and India abstained in the vote to condemn Moscow's action at the UN Security Council.

- China over the past decade engaged in a project of land reclamation in the South China Sea in violation of international law to advance its territorial claims and gain control of vital sea lanes.[27]

- China became much more activist, assertive, and strategic in multilateral organizations to dilute criticism of its human rights record and to weaken international norms of human rights, transparency, and accountability.[28]

- China used its geoeconomic leverage to coerce other countries into adopting Chinese technology (Huawei's 5G wireless network equipment) and to remain silent about its human rights abuses (including the largest internment of an ethnic or religious minority since World War II), repressive internal affairs, and increasingly aggressive foreign policies.[29]

- China chose to operate outside the framework of the international economic order, largely ignoring World Bank and even Asian Infrastructure

Investment Bank standards in its Belt and Road Initiative, which has grown to an estimated $1 trillion.[30]

- Russia cooperated with the Syrian regime to inflict mass atrocities on Syrian civilians, a dramatic departure from its general support or acquiescence in UN actions to prevent such human catastrophes in the post–Cold War period.[31]

- Russia in an unprecedented act interfered in the 2016 U.S. presidential election on behalf of Donald Trump and has continued massive interference in U.S. social media since.[32] In the wake of the COVID-19 pandemic, China has begun to adopt more assertive disinformation operations.[33]

- Several U.S. allies also diverged from world order. Hungary's democracy has withered under the rule of Prime Minister Viktor Orban. Turkey has become an authoritarian state. Saudi Arabia's crown prince ended decades of cautious foreign policies largely deferential to U.S. preferences in favor of a violent alternative and humanitarian catastrophe in Yemen.[34]

These actions are major departures from the shared understandings of the 1990s, and the return of great power rivalry shattered hopes in that multilateral order.[35] China and Russia in particular defend a Westphalian and nineteenth-century model of order organized around balance of power, national sovereignty, and spheres of influence.[36] They oppose the U.S. model of humanitarian intervention, democracy promotion, strengthened alliances, and opposition to spheres of influence. Meanwhile, the United States distances itself from its own world order traditions. President Trump questions the value of U.S. alliances, imposes trade tariffs on friend and foe alike, abandons support for human rights and democracy overseas, and pulled out of the Joint Comprehensive Plan of Action (the Iran nuclear deal), the Trans-Pacific Partnership (TPP), the Intermediate-Range Nuclear Forces Treaty, and the Paris climate change accord.[37] This approach could be reversed in the U.S. presidential election in November, but the United States currently contests its own liberal order. This did not start with Trump. The invasion of Iraq and the overly generous admission of China into the WTO were also serious mistakes that undermined the integrity of the liberal order—the first immediately and the second gradually.

The shifting preferences of the great powers have not been the only factor contributing to the demise of world order.

A TRANSITIONAL MOMENT

Almost every generation since World War II believed it was living in a period of radical change: the atomic threat of the 1950s, the leftist revolutionary thrusts of the 1960s and early 1970s, the microchip and information technology advances of the 1980s, globalization and the end of the Soviet Empire of the 1990s, and the rise of China, social media, and mass terrorism of the 2000s. However, except in the case of the end of the Soviet Union and the liberation of Eastern Europe, the fundamentals of international power, behavior, and influence have remained relatively constant. This time, there are reasons to believe that the dramatic changes underway in today's societies are ushering in a profoundly different era. New technologies in artificial intelligence and biological science as well as the internet and social media are changing how people work and consume information. These changes challenge some of the very structures of our society that have been in place since the late nineteenth century.

This upheaval was already well underway before COVID-19. The means of production, the delivery of services, the nature of education, the rules and practices of international trade, the threats to public order, the character of energy and environmental issues, and the entire meaning of balance of power were all already undergoing deep change. Traumas often catalyze, even accelerate, trends, and so it is with COVID-19. As this crisis evolves, it changes societies at micro and macro levels in ways most individuals cannot understand, much less shape. Layer on top of this the pressing international challenges— how to integrate these new technologies and mitigate their negative effects; how to deal with transnational dangers such as pandemic disease, terrorism, and the spread of nuclear weapons; how to reduce the long-term threat of climate change; how to ensure that the global economy produces more benefits and equities than vulnerabilities to the middle classes; and how to respond to the rise of China without destabilizing confrontation.

What does all of this add up to? The world order of the 1990s and early 2000s was rooted in U.S.-led postwar preferences, objectives, and strategies, which were adjusted and further globalized by their successors. To the extent that the major powers agreed on the constraints, limits, and enforcement mechanisms, the world order protected that international system. But now supporters of the old order, including many Americans, should grapple with the implications of shifting balances of power and the transformation of societies.

It is not so much that the major powers seek to directly overturn the old order; it is that in many respects the new world and the old rules are in parallel universes. For example, the Belt and Road Initiative does not seek to overturn the World Bank; it simply operates alongside it. As political scientists Alexander Cooley and Daniel Nexon note, "Regimes from around the world are unlikely, for better or for worse, to simply accept the kind of liberal ordering that the United States promoted in the 1990s and 2000s."[38]

The world has moved away from a standard of world order in which nations work within the same set of constraints and aspire to meet the same set of rules toward a model in which many countries choose their own paths to order, without much reference to the views of others, both near and far. This heterogeneity is not so much a rush to excellence as the projection of the domestic characteristics of the major powers into the international arena. Thus, the corruption, lack of accountability, and absence of freedom in autocratic countries is their version of order. Unbound from alliances and institutions, the vagaries of American domestic politics manifest themselves in unilateralist approaches to order. An application of Kissinger's model of world order is nowhere to be seen.

THE ROAD FORWARD

The fundamental strategic problem the United States faces with respect to world order is how it should respond to the breakdown in agreed arrangements between the major powers. The United States has a choice. Should it try to reconstitute a world order whereby it forges an understanding with Europe, Japan, India, China, and Russia on the limits of acceptable behavior and how to enforce them, or should it concentrate on improving its own ordering options in accordance with its values regardless of whether China, Russia, or others go along? The answer rests on which course of action best protects and advances U.S. vital national interests.

We define the country's vital interests as follows:[39]

- Prevent the use and reduce the threat of nuclear, biological, and chemical weapons and catastrophic conventional terrorist attacks or cyberattacks against the United States, its military forces abroad, or its allies.

- Prevent the spread of nuclear weapons, secure nuclear weapons and materials, and reduce further proliferation of intermediate- and long-range delivery systems for nuclear weapons.

- Maintain a global and regional balance of power that promotes peace, stability, and freedom through domestic U.S. robustness, U.S. international power and influence, and the strength of U.S. alliance systems, with increased contributions from allies and partners.

- Prevent the emergence of hostile major powers or failed states on U.S. borders.

- Ensure the viability and stability of major global systems (trade, financial markets, energy supplies, cyberspace, the environment, and freedom of the seas).

On the face of it, the answer would seem obvious: the United States should try to reconstitute a shared strategic understanding between the major powers based on these national interests—a classic world order bargain, if you will. But such a pathway is problematic. Although it may seem strategically sensible and prudent to many observers, for others the gap between the United States and China is too large to bridge, and a compromise could undermine Washington's regional alliances. Moreover, there is for the foreseeable future no appetite in Washington on either side of the aisle, or in Beijing, for such a comprehensive effort. The U.S. executive branch and Congress are focused on drawing up bills of indictment against China (many justified), with no prescriptive suggestion except for public coercion that diplomacy, difficult as it may be, could ease the bilateral tension. Opinion polls show that the American people favor alliances, free trade, and a foreign policy that includes support for human rights, democracy, and the rule of law.[40] With U.S. treatment of China a major issue in the 2020 presidential campaign, it is difficult to imagine a national consensus on any dramatic change of course that accommodates to some degree China's preferences regarding world order.

For its part, China seeks to comprehensively undermine U.S. alliances and to eventually replace the United States as both the most important power in Asia and the world's technological leader. Beijing is making progress in that long-term effort, as its coercive power grows and Washington falters internationally. Whatever the objective reality, Beijing's behavior suggests it could well believe it is playing a winning hand.

In any case, both nations at present are fully committed to their core convictions of how best to conduct their societies and governance, promote their national interests, and organize the international system. It is difficult to imagine either side offering major compromises on any of these fundamentals anytime soon.

The unfortunate condition of world order does not mean an end to order, or to narrow U.S.-China cooperation. The United States should ensure that the order it offers is as attractive to other nations as possible and is competitive with the alternatives offered by China or others. Washington should reinvigorate the ambition and scope of its great power diplomacy, using opportunities presented by a more multipolar world. This will require major changes to U.S. foreign policy as it has been practiced since the Cold War.

RECOMMENDATIONS

The United States finds itself in a world where there is little prospect that the major powers will converge on a single model of world order—with a shared understanding of constraints, limits, and the means of enforcement—as it has hoped for much of the past thirty years. It is also unlikely, though not impossible, that the international system will return to an informal construct of world order of the sort Europe practiced from 1815 to 1848. Rather, as in the Bismarck period, Americans should expect China, Russia, and several others to pursue their own ordering strategies, both in their regions and on global issues. Some grand bargains in world order could be struck in the distant future, but they appear remote now. The question is: What can and should the United States do to preserve its national interests and its own notion of international order in this uncertain environment?

The United States should not go back to the concept of the liberal international order (LIO).[41] The LIO is a relatively recent invention and is analytically distinct from its antecedents in the Atlantic Charter through to the creation of NATO. The term did not exist during the Cold War—when "the Free World" or "the West" was used to describe the U.S.-led bloc of nations—and was coined by political scientists in the 1990s. The substance of the LIO is admirable and worth preserving, but it also has several downsides. It reduces U.S. foreign policy to an abstract set of principles that are often violated. There is little sign that it resonates with the public, meaning it can be easily cast aside. The LIO also has embedded within it universal aspirations that have been dashed because of shifts in Chinese and Russian intentions as well as those of middle powers such as Brazil and Turkey.

Only an international order based on the enduring values of freedom and liberty can gain the sustained support of Congress and the

American people, but sadly John Winthrop's shining "City Upon a Hill" is currently dark. The United States should rebuild the core coalition of like-minded liberal democratic states as it did in the late 1940s, though with somewhat less military emphasis, and increase that partnership's resilience to solve the new challenges that free societies face. However, there would be at least one significant difference to the early days of the Cold War before détente: recognizing interdependence, this bloc should seriously engage its rivals and competitors, particularly on shared challenges such as climate change, nuclear proliferation, pandemics, international terrorism, genocide, and the global economy.

Specifically, we recommend the following:

Create a Persuasive Model of Competent U.S. Governance, Which Will in Turn Reinforce America's International Leadership. The COVID-19 crisis has laid bare a governance gap between the United States and other democracies. Whereas Germany, New Zealand, South Korea, Taiwan, and others have been able to mobilize the state to conduct massive testing, the United States has fallen far behind. Its failings are not just on public health. It is gaining a reputation as a dysfunctional superpower—one unable to pass budgets, manage its debt, ratify treaties, or carry out a coherent and consistent foreign policy. This dysfunction saps the will of the American public to play a leadership role in the world and reduces the legitimacy of American power overseas. Moreover, continued dysfunction will put the United States at a distinct strategic disadvantage vis-à-vis China. Initial domestic steps toward more competent democratic governance include investing more in education, fixing a broken immigration system, rooting out corruption, providing a role for the state in developing and deploying advanced technologies such as 5G, and predictably and adequately resourcing the federal government. Most of these are not new problems, but they are now more urgent than in recent memory. If these weaknesses in the quality of U.S. governance are not successfully addressed, Washington's capacity to influence other nations will continue to erode.

Reanimate American Diplomacy by Wielding Leverage More Effectively. U.S. global leadership is crucial to international peace and stability. For the past twenty years, the United States has failed to blend leverage and diplomacy in pursuit of its geopolitical goals. On some occasions, the United States acquired massive leverage but failed to convert it into a diplomatic victory (such as in 2003, when the threat of the use of force compelled Saddam Hussein to let inspectors back into Iraq). On other occasions, the United States engaged in intensive diplomacy but without any real leverage (as in the 2014–15 effort to bring about Israeli-Palestinian peace). There have been some exceptions—the negotiation of the 2015 Joint Comprehensive Plan of Action (JCPOA) with Iran—but the United States should reach beyond sanctions and find new ways of using its national power to create diplomatic opportunities. For instance, the United States should make military assistance to Saudi Arabia more contingent on Saudi behavior. It should, working with its allies, rejoin the JCPOA and open up a bilateral diplomatic dialogue with Iran. It should join the European Union to put pressure on Hungary to reverse its slide toward authoritarianism. It should use the threat of additional sanctions against North Korea to work with China to kick-start a genuine diplomatic process to limit Pyongyang's nuclear program. It should use the space and friction generated by a multipolar world to its advantage—for instance, rather than trying to outbid Beijing on global development projects, Washington could support the legitimate desire of people around the world for accountability and good governance to push back against Beijing's corrupt economic practices. And it should exploit the possibility to de-escalate some conflicts as their parties focus on the domestic consequences of the coronavirus crisis.

Revitalize North American Collaboration. The United States should invigorate its relations with Canada and Mexico, building on the strength of three continent-spanning democracies with five hundred million people, favorable demographics, and vast energy resources to its economic and security advantage on the global stage. As supply chains shift from China, the United States and these neighbors should amplify the recent U.S.-Mexico-Canada Agreement, invest in North American infrastructure, and promote an expanded role for North American multilateral banks to increase the flow of trade on the continent. Washington should coordinate with these neighbors on shared plans for organizations such as a restructured TPP, the Group of Twenty, and the Asia-Pacific Economic Cooperation forum. On the security front, the United States and Canada should work on a joint strategy for the Arctic—the great power threat that comes closest to American borders. To address immigration—among the most volatile issues in U.S. domestic politics—as well as organized crime and narcotics, this trilateral group should take cooperative action, including to bolster the rule of law and development in Mexico and make it easier for companies to hire professionals and low-skill seasonal workers from any of the three countries.[42] There is, of course, no guarantee that such an approach would be accepted in Mexico City, but, as hockey legend Wayne Gretzky said, "You miss 100 percent of the shots you don't take."

Fundamentally Reform the Way the United States Deals With Its Treaty Allies and Partners. No longer can Washington rely on its global and regional dominance to usually get its way. No longer can the United States routinely ignore the views of important like-minded states and still achieve policy success. No longer can the United States sometimes avoid substantial compromise if it wishes to bring others along with its diplomatic preferences. It is difficult to exaggerate the fundamental U.S. change of mind and practice that will be required to implement this revolutionary approach toward its allies and partners. Washington should on occasion accept "no" or "do it another way" as an answer from allies, difficult as that can be. For example, the United States should welcome the EU's initiative to deepen its defense cooperation; recognize that NATO enlargement to Georgia and Ukraine will not happen in the next four years, while keeping the door open for Sweden and Finland to join immediately should they wish to do so; and listen sympathetically to allied strategies regarding relations with Iran. The United States has an enormous advantage with the added capacities of its alliances, but one that Trump persistently undermines. It is unclear how long it will take the next president to reestablish trust among U.S. allies, but progress is unlikely to be rapid.[43]

Increase Ambitions With Europe. The United States and its European allies should be more ambitious and proactive if liberalism is to be a competitive force in world affairs. Over the past seventy years, the transatlantic alliance has been dogged by squabbles over level of defense spending, and now it is extremely unlikely that most European nations will ever make the 2 percent of gross domestic product (GDP) target.[44] The Transatlantic Trade and Investment Partnership was meant to provide a positive vision for the relationship, but it only ever offered a small increase in GDP (0.5 of 1 percent for the EU and 0.4 of 1 percent for the United States).[45] To be relevant, the alliance should address big issues that directly affect people's lives—agreed rules on data and the regulation of big technology, formal cooperation on developing and deploying new technologies such as 5G and artificial intelligence, and a common approach to the economic and political challenge from China. There are still questions around whether NATO's European member states and the EU have the will and ability to defend themselves from hard power threats. Shaping the international order on these issues is overwhelmingly in their vital interests, however, and they have the capacity to play this role.

Strengthen Relations With India. India, the world's largest democracy, promises to be a crucial U.S. partner. New Delhi is convinced that China seeks to replace the United States as the primary power in Asia, that this would be exceedingly bad for India, and that only a strong partnership with the United States can prevent it.[46] Washington and New Delhi should remember that their chief objective is not consensus on trade or Iran but contending with a rising China. The United States should take care regarding its demands on Indian foreign policy, when vital U.S. national interests are not at stake, when those demands undermine balancing China, and when they relate to peripheral differences in the bilateral relationship. India should accelerate defense cooperation with the United States and pursue reforms that allow more U.S. access to the Indian economy. Progress toward balancing China will be worth disagreements on other issues.

Advance International Cooperation on COVID-19 Treatments and Vaccines. Political philosopher John Rawls wrote about a veil of ignorance whereby a person should design how the world should work without knowing their station within it—whether they would be born poor or wealthy, male or female, white or black. Today, in the early stages of the COVID-19 crisis, no one knows which country or actor will develop a vaccine or treatments first. It could be the United States, but it could also be a military-linked laboratory in China or somewhere else entirely. Now is the time for the United States and all other nations to agree, under this veil of ignorance, how a vaccine and treatments should be distributed and managed once they are developed.[47] It would be a fitting and practical way to advance international cooperation in response to the worst global crisis since World War II. This agreement would require China to be substantially more transparent than it was in the early weeks of the coronavirus crisis.

Invest in International Institutions. Democratic administrations tend to work within international institutions as they are or to push for reforms to bring in rising powers. Some Republican administrations, particularly the Trump administration, are more likely to disengage from these institutions or to withdraw funding if they do not get their way. Both approaches are inadequate. China has been particularly active in multilateral organizations. Its influence in the World Health Organization (WHO) during the coronavirus crisis has caused an international scandal, and Beijing now heads up four of fifteen UN agencies—the International Civil Aviation Organization, the International Telecommunication Union, the Food and Agriculture Organization, and the Industrial Development Organization.[48] The answer to this challenge is for the United States to fully engage in and come up with a modernized vision of multilateral organizations. For example, the United States should work with democracies and other interested parties to address the imbalances in favor of China at the WTO, consider the concept of a "climate club" that would mandate a different incentive structure for nations to reduce greenhouse gases, and take a leading role to reform the WHO.[49]

Compartmentalize Transnational Challenges Such as Climate Change, Pandemics, and International Terrorism. The United States and China share certain interests in combating climate change and pandemic disease. These shared interests are jeopardized by the geopolitical competition between the two. For instance, the rivalry currently makes the prospect of cooperation on COVID-19 remote. However, rivals should be capable of cooperation on such matters. During the Cold War, the United States and the Soviet Union cooperated on managing their own nuclear weapons, the nuclear nonproliferation treaty, a vaccine to eliminate smallpox, fisheries, and freedom of the seas. To replicate that cooperation, the United States and China should compartmentalize these shared problems so that they are hermetically sealed from the overall relationship. Each side should make it clear to their publics that they will cooperate on climate, pandemics, nuclear proliferation, cyberspace, and the global economy, even as they compete ferociously in other domains. This will be exceedingly difficult to accomplish, but it should be the objective. If compartmentalizing proves impossible and the United States and China cannot work together on shared challenges, Washington should mitigate the risks of inaction by doing what it can with its allies and partners. For example, if China refuses to fully cooperate on pandemics, the United States should work with Australia, Japan, South Korea, Taiwan, the European Union, and others to share information, coordinate policies, and pool resources.

Stop Deterioration in the Balance of Power With China. For an intensified high-level bilateral dialogue between Washington and Beijing to be fruitful, the United States should first clearly establish that it is enhancing its military, diplomatic, and economic power projection into

Asia; increasing interaction with allies, partners, and friends; and help-
ing build up its allies' diplomatic, economic, and military strength. This
would mean, inter alia, that the United States should stop beating up
on its Asian allies. Successful diplomacy depends on deployable assets,
and Washington needs to increase its assets. Nothing less will convince
Beijing—which pursues classic realist policies based on the balance of
power—that it has reasons, based on its national interests, to negotiate
seriously with the United States. This will take some time, for Beijing
will wait to see whether Washington becomes distracted and diverts its
attention to other, lesser issues in the daily headlines, as is its wont.[50]

Compete With China. Even if the United States stops the deterioration
of the balance of power, Washington and Beijing are destined to be strategic competitors for the foreseeable future. The question is what type
of competition there will be. There can be no early return to a convergence strategy in the belief that the Chinese Communist Party regime
will become a responsible stakeholder in the U.S. order. Xi has been
clear that Beijing has its own vision of global order that he refers to as
"a community of common destiny," which is more ominous than the
previous formulation of "a harmonious world."[51] The Trump administration's approach is not a sustainable option either. The United States
currently appears to be headed for a full-throated permanent confrontation with China, with little diplomacy, constraints, limits, or prospects
of cooperation. The volatile piece of the relationship at present is not
security competition, which has been relatively stable and predictable.
The problem concerns the vulnerabilities created by interdependence
including the timing, shape, and substance of the next U.S.-China trade
agreement. The United States should devise a strategy toward China
that defines the scale and shape of engagement. Fully coordinated with
allies, this needs to be carefully designed and pay particular attention to
trade and finance, including joining a reconstituted TPP, international
institutions and frameworks, technology transfer, defense, cyber, critical infrastructure such as communications and energy, and development and investment controls. Without such intense collaboration, it
seems unlikely that the United States can successfully and peacefully
compete with China, which is likely to be a preeminent U.S. strategic
challenger for many decades. Inherent U.S. pessimism about this competition is misplaced. With the proper policies, the United States and its
allies can successfully compete with China while avoiding combustible
competition and defending alliance national interests and values.

Reduce Engagement in the Middle East. The COVID-19 crisis ought
to mark the end of the post-9/11 era.[52] The United States has overly
invested in the greater Middle East, and Washington should stop
trying to fix the most dysfunctional and self-destructive region on
earth. It is time to withdraw U.S. combat troops from Afghanistan
in the next year without requiring agreement with the Taliban; recognize that the possibility of a two-state solution to the Israel-Pales-
tine issue is more remote by the day; end support for the Saudi war in
Yemen; revive and update the JCPOA to prevent Tehran from acquiring nuclear weapons; be clear that, although the United States hopes
Iran becomes a democracy, that is a decision for the Iranian people,
and the United States should not be actively trying to bring this about;
and downgrade U.S. relations with its Arab partners, to focus on matters of mutual interest rather than offering general support for their
domestic and international objectives. While continuing its enduring commitment to Israel's safety and security, the United States
should redirect its resources from the Middle East to matters that are
far more relevant to its national interests today and in the future. It
should deal with the rise of Chinese power, deepen its relationships
with allies in Asia and Europe, seek major advances in new technologies, and tackle transnational threats such as climate change and pandemics. This shift should be done gradually, in concert with European
allies, to avoid a vacuum in the region; indeed, the EU should assume
more of the burden in attempting to shape the Middle East, which so
affects its vital national interests. This will be a heavy lift.

Condition Engagement With Russia. U.S. relations with Russia are at a
post–Cold War low. There is virtually no diplomacy between Washington and Moscow. Russia's interference in the U.S. election of 2016, its
aggressive acts in the Middle East since 2015, and its continuing aggres-
sion in Ukraine make meaningful cooperation currently improbable.
If Russia interferes in the 2020 U.S. election, the next administration
should impose additional and significant costs on Putin's regime and
inform Moscow that this will be the case. However, if Russia is judged
to have stayed out of the election, and if there is progress on ending Russian actions against Ukraine, there could be scope for a strategic dialogue with Russia that would explore ways of increasing cooperation on
shared interests, even as the two countries compete vigorously in other
domains. In any case, Washington should continue its negotiations with
Moscow on nuclear weapons.[53]

Rebuild but Reform the Global Economy. There is little doubt that the world is in the early stages of a protracted economic downturn. The only saving grace so far has been swift and massive action by the Federal Reserve and the European Central Bank, but tough days lie ahead. The United States should work with other countries so that the rebuilding of national economies is consistent with maintaining an open and mutually beneficial global economy. At the same time, the United States should also press for reforms to reduce the risk of future financial crises, change the international tax code so corporations pay tax somewhere, level the economic playing field between democracies and China's mercantilist model, tackle structural inequality, and ensure that free societies are collectively resilient and not dependent on rival powers for critical technologies and supplies.

CONCLUSION

The most immediate task facing the United States and the world is the COVID-19 crisis and its aftermath. The next administration's most important task will be to craft and shepherd a cooperative international response on the production of a vaccine and treatments, coordinate the rebuilding of national economies so they reinforce a mutually beneficial global economy, assist developing countries disproportionately weakened by the virus, and reform global institutions and infrastructure so they are better positioned to deal with the next pandemic and international challenges as a whole. There is a real danger that the United States and other nations will pursue a nationalist beggar-thy-neighbor approach that could damage their national interests as well as global peace and prosperity in a way that will be impossible to recover from in the short to medium term. As a result, tackling coronavirus globally ought to be Washington's top foreign policy priority.

The focus of this report is to look beyond COVID-19 and to address the troubling divergence between how the major powers conceive of world order. The fault lines that emerged in the past decade have now become a chasm and have stripped away any illusion that major power convergence is possible. There is no prospect of a Kissingerian world order in the foreseeable future. Take sovereignty as an example. After the Cold War, many nations led by the United States agreed that national sovereignty was contingent on a government's operating without brutality within its borders. Today, China, Russia, and others reject this concept. With an absolutist interpretation of sovereign rights, they publicly espouse no external interference under any circumstances. Thus, there will be no shared international understanding of this fundamental principle.

The challenges the United States currently confronts are daunting, but no more so than those faced by many earlier generations of Americans. Avoiding dangerous confrontations with rivals is possible, but only if the United States is up to that diplomatic challenge, based on U.S. national interests and democratic values. Through wise and steady international leadership, Washington can also implement adroit and consistent policies that substantially shape international order in line with its preferences and perhaps that eventually move toward the noble world order concept. With COVID-19, the reordering moment is here.

ENDNOTES

1. Lawrence Summers, "Covid-19 Looks Like a Hinge in History," *Financial Times*, May 14, 2020, http://ft.com/content/de643ae8-9527-11ea-899a-f62a20d54625.

2. "Coronavirus Resource Center," Johns Hopkins University and Medicine, accessed May 1, 2020, http://coronavirus.jhu.edu/map.html.

3. *World Economic Outlook, April 2020: The Great Lockdown* (Washington, DC: International Monetary Fund, April 2020), http://imf.org/en/Publications/WEO /Issues/2020/04/14/weo-april-2020.

4. Maria Abi-Habib, "Millions Had Risen Out of Poverty. Coronavirus Is Pulling Them Back.," *New York Times*, April 30, 2020, http://nytimes.com/2020/04/30/world /asia/coronavirus-poverty-unemployment.html; Emma Graham, "IMF Warns 'Vulnerabilities High' in the Middle East Hit With Dual Shock of Coronavirus and Oil Plunge," CNBC, April 15, 2020, http://cnbc.com/2020/04/15/imf-warns -vulnerabilities-high-in-the-middle-east-hit-with-dual-shock-of-coronavirus-and-oil -plunge.html; Tony Romm and Jeff Stein, "2.4 Million Americans Filed Jobless Claims Last Week, Bringing Nine-Week Total to 38.6 Million," *Washington Post*, May 21, 2020, http://washingtonpost.com/business/2020/05/21/unemployment-claims -coronavirus; and Matina Stevis-Gridneff and Jack Ewing, "EU Is Facing Its Worst Recession Ever. Watch Out, World.," *New York Times*, May 6, 2020, http://nytimes .com/2020/05/06/business/coronavirus-europe-reopening-recession.html.

5. Economists expect a prolonged recovery. See Clive Crook, "About That V-Shaped Recovery," Bloomberg, April 28, 2020, http://bloomberg.com/opinion/articles/2020 -04-28/v-shaped-economic-recovery-from-coronavirus-is-not-happening; Chris Giles, "Economists Question BOE's Overly Rosy View of V-Shaped Recovery," *Financial Times*, May 7, 2020, http://ft.com/content/4fd6f037-ac00-4cb6-9d1e-42283fc4ca31; Andy Kessler, "What Shape Will the Rebound Take?," *Wall Street Journal*, April 26, 2020, http://wsj.com/articles/what-shape-will-the-rebound-take-11587930592; David J. Lynch, "Soaring Joblessness Could Shake U.S. Economy, Politics for Years," *Washington Post*, May 8, 2020, http://washingtonpost.com/business/2020/05/08/jobs -coronavirus-unemployment-economy-politics; and Ann Saphir, "No 'V'-Shape Return From Devastating U.S. Job Loss, Fed Policymakers Say," Reuters, May 8, 2020, http://reuters.com/article/us-health-coronavirus-fed-daly/no-v-shape-return-from

-devastating-us-job-loss-fed-policymakers-say-idUSKBN22K30P. Health experts predict the pandemic will last for at least a year. A V-shaped recovery is unrealistic given the social and economic disruption associated with this timeline. Helen Branswell, "Americans Are Underestimating How Long Coronavirus Disruptions Will Last, Health Experts Say," STAT, April 3, 2020, http://statnews.com/2020/04/03/americans-are-underestimating-how-long-coronavirus-disruptions-will-last-health-experts-say; Juliette Kayyem, "The Crisis Could Last 18 Months. Be Prepared.," *Atlantic*, March 21, 2020, http://theatlantic.com/ideas/archive/2020/03/there-isnt-going-be-all-clear-signal/608512; Christina Larson and Michelle R. Smith, "How Long Will Americans Be Fighting the Coronavirus?," Associated Press, March 19, 2020, http://apnews.com/67ac94d1cf08a84ff7c6bbeec2b167fa; Kristine A. Moore, Marc Lipsitch, John M. Barry, and Michael T. Osterholm, "COVID-19: The CIDRAP Viewpoint," Center for Infectious Disease Research and Policy, April 30, 2020, http://cidrap.umn.edu/sites/default/files/public/downloads/cidrap-covid19-viewpoint-part1_0.pdf; and Matt Stieb, "U.S. Coronavirus Plan Warns Pandemic 'Will Last 18 Months or Longer,'" *New York Magazine*, March 18, 2020, http://nymag.com/intelligencer/2020/03/u-s-coronavirus-plan-pandemic-will-last-over-18-months.html.

6. For those less timid, see Richard Haass, "The Pandemic Will Accelerate History Rather than Reshape It," *Foreign Affairs*, April 7, 2020, http://foreignaffairs.com/articles/united-states/2020-04-07/pandemic-will-accelerate-history-rather-reshape-it; Joseph S. Nye Jr., "No, the Coronavirus Will Not Change the Global Order," *Foreign Policy*, April 16, 2020, http://foreignpolicy.com/2020/04/16/coronavirus-pandemic-china-united-states-power-competition; Daniel W. Drezner, "The Most Counterintuitive Prediction About World Politics and the Coronavirus," *Washington Post*, March 30, 2020, http://washingtonpost.com/outlook/2020/03/30/most-counterintuitive-prediction-about-world-politics-covid-19; Kurt M. Campbell and Rush Doshi, "The Coronavirus Could Reshape Global Order: China Is Maneuvering for International Leadership as the United States Falters," *Foreign Affairs*, March 18, 2020, http://foreignaffairs.com/articles/2020-03-18/coronavirus-could-reshape-global-order; Michael Green and Evan S. Medeiros, "The Pandemic Won't Make China the World's Leader: Few Countries Are Buying the Model or the Message From Beijing," *Foreign Affairs*, April 15, 2020, http://foreignaffairs.com/articles/united

-states/2020-04-15/pandemic-wont-make-china-worlds-leader; Colin H. Kahl and Ariana Berengaut, "Aftershocks: The Coronavirus Pandemic and the New World Disorder," *War on the Rocks*, April 10, 2020, http://warontherocks.com/2020/04 /aftershocks-the-coronavirus-pandemic-and-the-new-world-disorder; Amitav Acharya, "How Coronavirus May Reshape the World Order," *National Interest*, April 18, 2020, http://nationalinterest.org/feature/how-coronavirus-may-reshape-world -order-145972; Salvatore Babones, "Don't Bash Globalization—It Will Rescue Our Economies After the Pandemic," *Foreign Policy*, April 25, 2020, http://foreignpolicy .com/2020/04/25/globalization-economic-recovery-coronavirus-pandemic; Nicholas Eberstadt, "The 'New Normal': Thoughts About the Shape of Things to Come in the Post-Pandemic World," National Bureau of Asian Research, April 18, 2020, http:// nbr.org/publication/the-new-normal-thoughts-about-the-shape-of-things-to-come-in -the-post-pandemic-world; Neil Irwin, "It's the End of the World Economy as We Know It," *New York Times*, April 16, 2020, http://nytimes.com/2020/04/16/upshot /world-economy-restructuring-coronavirus.html; and Minxin Pei, "China's Coming Upheaval: Competition, the Coronavirus, and the Weakness of Xi Jinping," *Foreign Affairs*, May/June 2020, http://foreignaffairs.com/articles/united-states/2020-04-03 /chinas-coming-upheaval.

7. See John M. Barry, *The Great Influenza: The Story of the Deadliest Pandemic in History* (New York: Penguin Books, 2005); and Laura Spinney, *Pale Rider: The Spanish Flu of 1918 and How It Changed the World* (New York: Public Affairs, 2017).

8. Richard Haass, "A Cold War With China Would Be a Mistake," *Wall Street Journal*, May 7, 2020, http://wsj.com/articles/dont-start-a-new-cold-war-with-china -11588860761; Javed Ali and A'ndre Gonawela, "Dueling COVID-19 Blame Narratives Deepen US-China Rift," *Hill*, April 23, 2020, http://thehill.com/opinion /national-security/494133-dueling-covid-19-blame-narratives-deepen-us-china-rift; Finbarr Bermingham and Cissy Zhou, "Coronavirus: China and US in 'New Cold War' as Relations Hit Lowest Point in 'More Than 40 Years', Spurred on By Pandemic," *South China Morning Post*, May 5, 2020, http://scmp.com/economy/china-economy /article/3082968/coronavirus-china-us-new-cold-war-relations-hit-lowest-point; Michael Crowley, Edward Wong, and Lara Jakes, "Coronavirus Drives the U.S. and China Deeper Into Global Power Struggle," *New York Times*, March 22, 2020, http:// nytimes.com/2020/03/22/us/politics/coronavirus-us-china.html; and Benjamin Wilhelm, "The Coronavirus Pandemic Is Pushing U.S.-China Relations to New Lows," *World Politics Review*, May 6, 2020, http://worldpoliticsreview.com/trend-lines/28740 /the-coronavirus-pandemic-is-pushing-u-s-china-relations-to-new-lows.

9. We do not use the term *cold war* regarding U.S.-China relations because we believe that competition is so different in character from that between the United States and the Soviet Union.

10. This did not mean that everywhere there was peace on earth. In this decade there was violence and upheaval in Somalia, Haiti, Rwanda, the Balkans, and the U.S. war with Iraq. Nevertheless, none of these episodes caused a crisis between the great powers.

11. T. S. Eliot, "Journey of the Magi," *Ariel Poems* (London: Faber and Faber, 2014).

12. For example, see Samuel Charap and Jeremy Shapiro, "Consequences of a New Cold War," *Survival* 57, no. 2 (April–May 2015): 37–46; Michael J. Boyle, "The Coming Illiberal Order," *Survival* 58, no. 2 (April–May 2016): 35–66; and Emile Simpson,

"This Is How the Liberal World Order Ends," *Foreign Policy*, February 19, 2016, http://foreignpolicy.com/2016/02/19/this-is-how-the-liberal-world-order-ends.

13. Robert Kagan, *The Jungle Grows Back: America and Our Imperiled World* (New York: Knopf, 2018).

14. For an optimistic take on the state of the world, see Michael A. Cohen and Micah Zenko, *Clear and Present Safety: The World Has Never Been Better and Why That Matters to Americans* (New Haven, CT: Yale University Press, 2019).

15. Henry A. Kissinger, *A World Restored: Metternich, Castlereagh, and the Problems of Peace 1812–22* (Auckland, NZ: Friedland Books, 1957), 2–3. Kissinger here uses the term *international order*, but his definition fits what he elsewhere describes as "world order."

16. Henry A. Kissinger, *World Order* (New York: Penguin Press, 2014), 9.

17. Paul W. Schroeder, *The Transformation of European Politics 1763–1848* (New York: Oxford University Press, 1994).

18. Henry A. Kissinger, "The White Revolutionary: Reflections on Bismarck," *Daedalus* 97, no. 3 (1968): 888–924.

19. G. John Ikenberry, *Liberal Leviathan: The Origins, Crisis, and Transformation of the American World Order* (Princeton, NJ: Princeton University Press, 2011).

20. Unipolarity is a concept in international relations literature defined as "an anarchical interstate system featuring a sole great power." See Nuno P. Monteiro, *Theory of Unipolar Politics* (New York: Cambridge University Press, 2014), 40. Another political scientist, Michael Beckley, states it even more plainly: "Unipolarity is not omnipotence; it simply means that the United States has more than twice the wealth and military capabilities of any nation." See *Unrivaled: Why America Will Remain the World's Sole Superpower* (Ithaca, NY: Cornell University Press, 2018).

21. *Balancing* is the term of art in political science to describe how one great power seeks to deliberately thwart another's strategy either by building up its own military or forging alliances. Russia, for example, opposed the U.S. invasion of Iraq but did not arm Saddam Hussein or intervene on his behalf—things that it would do in Syria in 2015. As China rose and Russia recovered, Russia gained the capacity to balance again and chose to exercise it. See G. John Ikenberry, ed., *America Unrivaled: The Future of the Balance of Power* (Ithaca, NY: Cornell University Press, 2002).

22. For an account of Russian foreign policy during this period, see Angela E. Stent, *The Limits of Partnership: U.S. – Russian Relations in the Twenty-First Century* (Princeton, NJ: Princeton University Press, 2015).

23. See, for instance, Jim O'Neill, *The Growth Map: Economic Opportunity in the BRICs and Beyond* (New York: Penguin Press, 2011).

24. One must wonder if this weakening of U.S. norms was partly caused by a shift in the balance of power at the expense of the United States and a period of uncertain American foreign policy.

25. Michael J. Abramowitz, *Freedom in the World 2018: Democracy in Crisis* (Washington, DC: Freedom House, 2018), http://freedomhouse.org/sites/default/files/FH_FITW _Report_2018_Final_SinglePage.pdf.

26. See Stein Ringen, *The Perfect Dictatorship: China in the 21st Century* (Hong Kong: HKU Press, 2016).

27. Asia Maritime Transparency Initiative, "China Lands First Bomber on South China Sea Island," Center for Strategic and International Studies, May 18, 2018, http://amti.csis .org/china-lands-first-bomber-south-china-sea-island; Richard Heydarian, "How the Scarborough Shoal Came Back to Haunt China-Philippines Relations," *South China Morning Post*, June 23, 2018, http://scmp.com/news/china/diplomacy-defence/article /2151923/how-scarborough-shoal-came-back-haunt-china-philippines; Lyle J. Morris, "Time to Speak Up About the South China Sea," RAND Corporation, March 20, 2019, http://rand.org/blog/2019/03/time-to-speak-up-about-the-south-china-sea.html; and Gregory Poling and Bonnie S. Glaser, "How the U.S. Can Step Up in the South China Sea: The Right Way to Push Back Against Beijing," *Foreign Affairs*, January 16, 2019, http://foreignaffairs.com/articles/china/2019-01-16/how-us-can-step-south-china-sea.

28. Ted Piccone, *China's Long Game on Human Rights at the United Nations* (Washington, DC: Brookings Institution, September 2018), http://brookings.edu/research/chinas -long-game-on-human-rights-at-the-united-nations.

29. For an extensive treatment of China's use of coercive geoeconomic instruments, see Robert D. Blackwill and Jennifer M. Harris, *War by Other Means: Geoeconomics and Statecraft* (Cambridge, MA: Harvard University Press, 2016).

30. Daniel R. Russel and Blake Berger, "Navigating the Belt and Road Initiative," Asia Society Policy Institute, June 2019, 7, http://asiasociety.org/sites/default/files/2019-06 /Navigating the Belt and Road Initiative_2.pdf.

31. Russia did block a UN Security Council resolution on Kosovo in 1999.

32. Robert S. Mueller III, *Report on the Investigation Into Russian Interference in the 2016 Presidential Election* (Washington, DC: U.S. Department of Justice, March 2019), http://justice.gov/storage/report.pdf.

33. Edward Wong, Matthew Rosenberg, and Julian E. Barnes, "Chinese Agents Helped Spread Messages That Sowed Virus Panic in U.S., Officials Say," *New York Times*, April 22, 2020, http://nytimes.com/2020/04/22/us/politics/coronavirus-china -disinformation.html.

34. The exception to this prolonged and cautious Saudi foreign policy was its financial support for terrorist groups in Pakistan.

35. Robert Keohane, the political scientist who founded the theory known as institutionalism or neoliberal institutionalism, is known as a champion of international cooperation. But it is often forgotten that in his theory he stipulated that cooperation in institutions only really worked when the interests of the major powers were compatible with each other. Institutions could help overcome distrust, and they could solve collective action problems. They could not convince one power to abandon its interests if it conflicted with another's. Thus, they were best suited to like-minded nations.

36. Interference in U.S. domestic discourse by the two is, of course, inconsistent with a Westphalian model.

37. Thomas Wright, "Trump's Foreign Policy Is No Longer Unpredictable," *Foreign Affairs*, January 18, 2019, http://foreignaffairs.com/articles/world/2019-01-18 /trumps-foreign-policy-no-longer-unpredictable.

38. Alexander Cooley and Daniel Nexon, *Exit from Hegemony: The Unraveling of the American Global Order* (New York: Oxford University Press, 2020), 187.

39. This rigorous definition of U.S. national interests has been developed over twenty-five years in an enduring conversation and partnership with Graham Allison. See Graham Allison and Robert Blackwill, *America's National Interests* (Washington, DC: Commission on America's National Interests, 2000), http://belfercenter.org/files/amernatinter.pdf.

40. Dina Smeltz, Ivo Daalder, Karl Friedhof, Craig Kafura, and Brendan Helm, *Rejecting Retreat: Americans Support U.S. Engagement in Global Affairs* (Chicago: Chicago Council on Global Affairs, September 2019), http://thechicagocouncil.org/publication/lcc/rejecting-retreat.

41. For the case for the liberal international order, see Ikenberry, *Liberal Leviathan*; and Bruce Jones, *Still Ours to Lead: America, Rising Powers, and the Tension Between Rivalry and Restraint* (Washington, DC: Brookings Institution, 2014). For the case against, see Patrick Porter, *The False Promise of Liberal Order* (Medford, MA: Polity Press, 2020); Stephen M. Walt, *The Hell of Good Intentions: America's Foreign Policy Elite and the Decline of U.S. Primacy* (New York: Farrar, Strauss and Giroux, 2018); John J. Mearsheimer, *The Great Delusion: Liberal Dreams and International Realities* (New Haven, CT: Yale University Press, 2018); and Barry R. Posen, *Restraint: A New Foundation for U.S. Grand Strategy* (Ithaca, NY: Cornell University Press, 2014).

42. For recommendations to this end, see Council on Foreign Relations, *North America: Time for a New Focus* (New York: Council on Foreign Relations, 2014), 70–78.

43. See Robert D. Blackwill, *Implementing Grand Strategy Toward China: Twenty-Two U.S. Policy Prescriptions* (New York: Council on Foreign Relations, 2020), 24, http://cdn.cfr.org/sites/default/files/report_pdf/CSR85_Blackwill_China.pdf.

44. Oddly, some European NATO member states could make the 2 percent target this year because of collapsing GDP, which just demonstrates the weakness of the target, but very quickly there will be significant downward pressure on the defense budget.

45. European Commission, *Trade SIA on the Transatlantic Trade and Investment Partnership (TTIP) Between the EU and the USA*, Draft Interim Technical Report, prepared by Ecorys, May 2016, http://trade-sia.com/ttip/wp-content/uploads/sites/6/2014/02/TSIA-TTIP-draft-Interim-Technical-Report.pdf.

46. Regarding Indian views of the China threat, see Robert D. Blackwill and Ashley J. Tellis, "The India Dividend: New Delhi Remains Washington's Best Hope in Asia," *Foreign Affairs*, September/October 2019, http://foreignaffairs.com/articles/india/2019-08-12/india-dividend.

47. Unfortunately, the Trump administration refused to join international discussions on the coronavirus vaccine. See William Booth, Carolyn Y. Johnson, and Carol Morello, "The World Came Together for a Virtual Vaccine Summit. The U.S. Was Conspicuously Absent.," *Washington Post*, May 4, 2020, http://washingtonpost.com/world/europe/the-world-comes-together-for-a-virtual-vaccine-summit-the-us-is-conspicuously-absent/2020/05/04/ac5b6754-8a5c-11ea-80df-d24b35a568ae_story.html.

48. Courtney J. Fung and Shing-Hon Lam, "China Already Leads 4 of the 15 U.N. Specialized Agencies—and Is Aiming for a 5th," *Washington Post*, March 3, 2020,

http://washingtonpost.com/politics/2020/03/03/china-already-leads-4-15-un
-specialized-agencies-is-aiming-5th.

49. William Nordhaus, "The Climate Club: How to Fix a Failing Global Effort," *Foreign Affairs*, May/June 2020, http://foreignaffairs.com/articles/united-states/2020-04-10/climate-club.

50. This prescription draws on Blackwill, *Implementing Grand Strategy Toward China: Twenty-Two U.S. Policy Prescriptions*, 41.

51. On this shift in China's intentions under Xi Jinping see Daniel Tobin, *How Xi Jinping's "New Era" Should Have Ended U.S. Debate on Beijing's Ambitions* (Washington, DC: Center for Strategic and International Studies, 2020), http://csis.org/analysis/how-xi-jinpings-new-era-should-have-ended-us-debate-beijings-ambitions.

52. See Martin Indyk, "The Middle East Isn't Worth It Anymore," *Wall Street Journal*, January 17, 2020, http://wsj.com/articles/the-middle-east-isnt-worth-it-anymore-11579277317.

53. Assuming that the Trump administration does not seek an extension, the New Strategic Arms Reduction Treaty (START) will expire weeks after the inauguration of the U.S. president in 2021. The new president should immediately begin talks with Russia to extend the treaty. If Russia interferes in the U.S. presidential election and the United States imposes new sanctions, Washington should reject any attempt by Moscow to link a nuclear arms control agreement to a softening of U.S. sanctions.

ABOUT THE AUTHORS

Robert D. Blackwill is the Henry A. Kissinger senior fellow for U.S. foreign policy at the Council on Foreign Relations. He is also the Diller-von Furstenberg Family Foundation distinguished scholar at the Henry A. Kissinger Center for Global Affairs at Johns Hopkins University's School of Advanced International Studies. He is a former deputy assistant to the president, deputy national security advisor for strategic planning, and presidential envoy to Iraq under President George W. Bush. He was U.S. ambassador to India from 2001 to 2003. In 2016 he became the first U.S. ambassador to India since John Kenneth Galbraith to receive the Padma Bhushan Award from the government of India for distinguished service of a high order. From 1989 to 1990, he was special assistant to President George H.W. Bush for European and Soviet affairs, during which he was awarded the Commander's Cross of the Order of Merit by the Federal Republic of Germany for his contribution to German unification. Earlier in his career, he was the U.S. ambassador to conventional arms negotiations with the Warsaw Pact, director for European affairs at the National Security Council, principal deputy assistant secretary of state for political-military affairs, and principal deputy assistant secretary of state for European affairs. Blackwill is the author and editor of many articles and books on transatlantic relations, Russia and the West, the greater Middle East, and Asian security. His latest book, *War by Other Means: Geoeconomics and Statecraft*, coauthored with Jennifer M. Harris, was named a best foreign policy book of 2016 by *Foreign Affairs*. He is the author of the Council Special Reports *Trump's Foreign Policies Are Better Than They Seem* (April 2019) and *Implementing Grand Strategy Toward China: Twenty-Two U.S. Policy Prescriptions* (January 2020).

Thomas Wright is the director of the Center on the United States and Europe and a senior fellow in the Project on International Order and Strategy at the Brookings Institution. He is also a contributing writer for the *Atlantic* and a nonresident fellow at the Lowy Institute for International Policy. He was previously executive director of studies at the Chicago Council on Global Affairs and a lecturer at the University of Chicago's Harris School of Public Policy. He is the author of *All Measures Short of War: The Contest for the 21st Century and the Future of American Power*, which was published by Yale University Press in May 2017. Wright has a doctorate from Georgetown University, a master of philosophy from Cambridge University, and a bachelor's and a master's from University College Dublin. He has also held a predoctoral fellowship at Harvard University's Belfer Center for Science and International Affairs and a postdoctoral fellowship at Princeton University.

www.ingramcontent.com/pod-product-compliance
Lightning Source LLC
Chambersburg PA
CBHW070818280326
41934CB00012B/3223